Hawaii
America's Paradise

Hawaii
America's Paradise

Barbara Paulding Thrasher
Featuring the photographs of Jeff Gnass

LONGMEADOW PRESS

A Bison Book

Page 1: A fern and bamboo forest in Akaka Falls State Park on the Big Island.

Pages 2-3: Crashing surf and muted sunset create a dramatic scene on the coast of Molokai.

This page: A tranquil sunset glimpsed from Waikiki Beach, with catamarans headed for port.

This edition produced exclusively for Waldenbooks by
Bison Books Corp.
17 Sherwood Place
Greenwich, CT 06830

ISBN 0-681-29911-8

Printed in Hong Kong

Acknowledgments

The author and publisher would like to thank the following people who have helped in the preparation of this book: Richard and Sonja Glassman, who designed it; Elizabeth M Montgomery, who edited it; John K Crowley and Mary Raho, who did the picture research.

Picture Credits
All photographs by Jeff Gnass, with the following exceptions:

Free Lance Photographers Guild: endpapers, 4-5, 6-7, 10-11, 14, 15 (top), 16-17, 21 (top left and top right), 22-23, 24, 25, 26-27, 27 (top), 30-31, 32, 33 (bottom), 34-35, 36, 38-39, 42, 57 (top), 60-61, 62 (upper left), 63 (right top and bottom), 64, 65, 67 (bottom), 70 (top), 73, 74-75, 78 (three on left), 79 (two on right), 82-83, 88-89, 90, 91 (bottom right), 93, 94-95.

Allan Seiden 27 (bottom).

Sheraton Public Relations Department 62 (lower left).

US Geologic Survey 8-9.

Contents

Introduction

Hawaii's long and colorful history began when the volcanoes first rose out of the sea, and life, borne by water and wind, was established. Lush vegetation and rugged beauty greeted the first human settlers – Polynesians who sailed from Tahiti about 750 AD, bringing their native foods and customs. Captain Cook's discovery of the islands in 1778 was soon followed by visits from traders, and whalers used the islands to resupply and enjoy the amenities. By the early 1800s King Kamehameha I had unified Hawaii by force, but the Protestant missionaries who arrived in 1820 taught the natives democracy as well as religion and agriculture. Conflicts between whalers and missionaries erupted as each saw the other corrupting 'their' islands, at the same time, disease brought by the white man was taking its toll on the native population, which declined from 300,000 in 1780 to 70,000 in 1851.

Pineapple and sugar cane brought big business to Hawaii as plantation owners imported Chinese and Japanese contract laborers to work the fields, establishing the interracial nature of Hawaii's population. Recognizing its economic as well as strategic importance, the United States annexed Hawaii in 1900. By the time the Japanese attack on Pearl Harbor brought Hawaii to world prominence, the foundations had been laid for statehood, which was achieved on 21 August 1959.

Each major island in Hawaii has its own particular flavor and spirit. Hawaii, the Big Island, boasts two active volcanoes, a national park, an abundance of flowers, cattle ranches, and skiing on both water and snow. Maui, the Valley Island, juxtaposes green valleys with the stark beauty of Haleakala. Molokai, the Friendly Island, preserves the old ways of life in its quiet and peaceful setting. Lanai, the Pineapple Island, remote and least-visited, is marked by a wild and windswept beauty. Honolulu, Diamond Head, Waikiki and many other focal points make Oahu, the main island, the hub of Hawaii. Kauai, the Garden Island, the first to be settled by the Polynesians, has beautiful beaches and verdant canyons.

The islands of Hawaii offer up their ever-changing beauty to all who seek it. Linking east and west, old and new, the Hawaiian Islands lie in the vast ocean like scattered, magical gems.

In Maui's Haleakala National Park, the Kalahaku Overlook offers a spectacular view. In the distance Hawaii's Mauna Kea juts above the clouds.

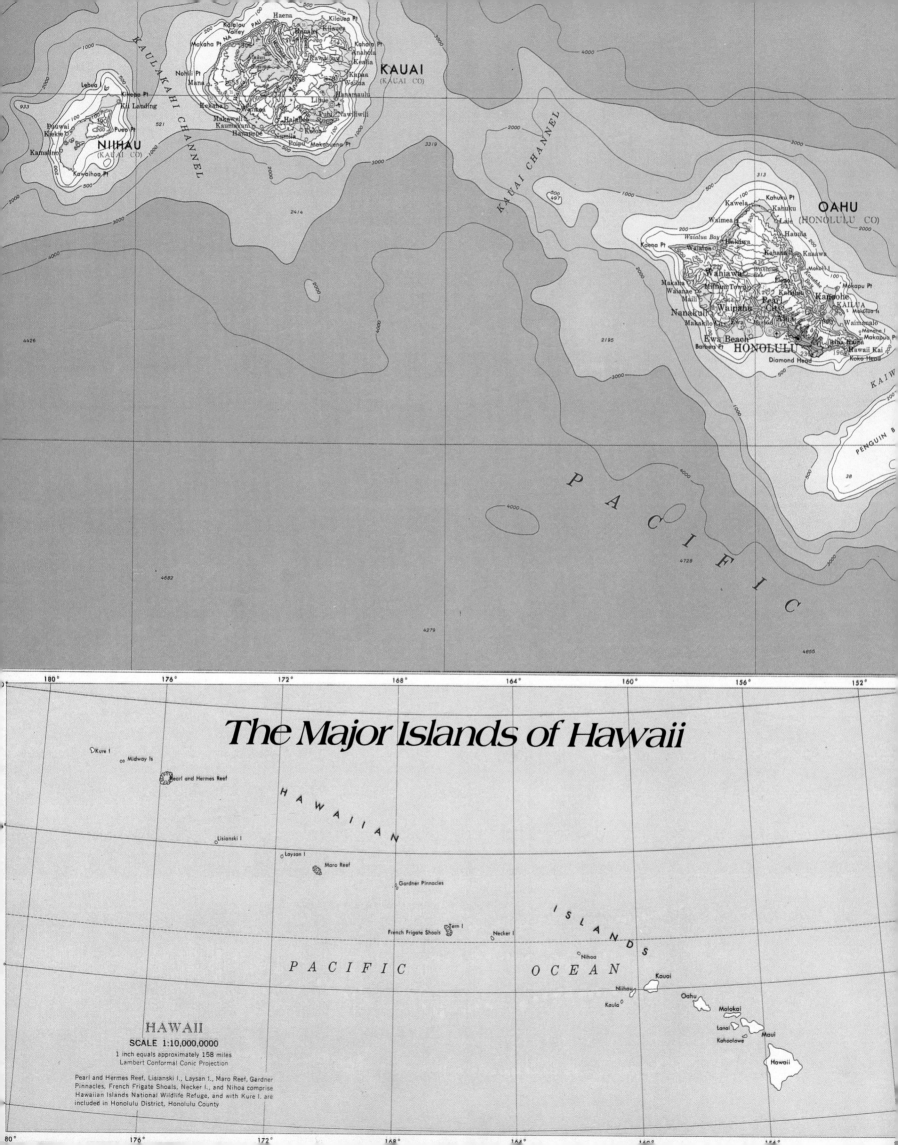

The Major Islands of Hawaii

KAULAKAHI CHANNEL

NIIHAU
(KAUAI CO)

KAUAI
(KAUAI CO)

KAUAI CHANNEL

OAHU
(HONOLULU CO)

HONOLULU

KAILUA

PACIFIC

KAIWI

PENGUIN B

HAWAIIAN

ISLANDS

PACIFIC   OCEAN

Kure I.
Midway Is
Pearl and Hermes Reef
Lisianski I.
Laysan I.
Maro Reef
Gardner Pinnacles
French Frigate Shoals
Tern I.
Necker I.
Nihoa
Kauai
Niihau
Kaula
Oahu
Molokai
Lanai
Maui
Kahoolawe
Hawaii

HAWAII

SCALE 1:10,000,0000

1 inch equals approximately 158 miles
Lambert Conformal Conic Projection

Pearl and Hermes Reef, Lisianski I., Laysan I., Maro Reef, Gardner
Pinnacles, French Frigate Shoals, Necker I., and Nihoa comprise
Hawaiian Islands National Wildlife Refuge, and with Kure I. are
included in Honolulu District, Honolulu County

Hawaii

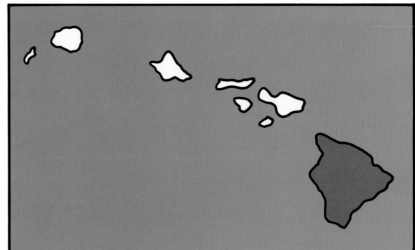

Hawaii

When the Reverand Hiram Bingham arrived in Hawaii in 1820 with the first missionary party, he was struck by the 'grandeur and beauty' of the island's 'verdant hills and deep ravines.' The missionaries landed at Kailua, the place from which the great King Kamehameha I had ruled over the islands he had united. Not far to the south, Captain Cook had landed, and later died in 1778. Steeped in history, Hawaii has many names: the Big Island, the Volcano Island, the Orchid Island. The largest, youngest, and southernmost island, Hawaii is composed of five volcanic mountains, two of which rise to an astounding height of 30,000 feet from the ocean floor. It is said that the ancient Hawaiian fire goddess, Pele, lives in Kilauea's Halemaumau Crater, from which she emerges now and again. Volcanoes National Park preserves the integrity of the fantastic volcanic landscape and the attendant, unusual wildlife.

About the size of Connecticut, the Big Island offers a diversity of scenery, from tropical rain forests to volcanic wasteland. Ruins of *heiaus*, the ancient Hawaiian temples where human sacrifice was practiced, can be found here. Cattle ranches, glorious fields of flowers both wild and cultivated, fruit-laden papaya and banana trees, rushing waterfalls, and the large but friendly city of Hilo all contribute to the variegated character of this lovely place. Mark Twain wrote the best description of the Hawaiian islands when he visited them in 1866, 'I saw on the one side a frame-work of tall, precipitous mountains close at hand, clad in refreshing green, and cleft by deep, cool, chasm-like valleys — and in front the grand sweep of the ocean: a brilliant, transparent green near the shore, bound and bordered by a long white line of foamy spray dashing against the reef, and further out the dead blue water of the deep sea, flecked with "white caps," and in the far horizon a single, lonely sail — a mere accent-mark to emphasize a slumberous calm and a solitude that were without sound or limit. When the sun sunk down — the one intruder from other realms and persistent in suggestions of them — it was tranced luxury to sit in the perfumed air and forget that there was any world but these enchanted islands.'

A ship moves along the horizon on a balmy afternoon in Kailua Bay on the Kona Coast. This is where the Protestant missionaries landed in 1820.

Pages 10-11: Coconut trees fringe the black sand beach of Kaimu on Hawaii's eastern shore, formed as molten lava met the ocean and exploded into pieces.

Opposite page: On the eastern shore of Hawaii, about 10 miles north of Hilo, the 66-acre arboretum called Akaka Falls State Park offers a lush forest of bamboo, ferns and giant gingers. Canopied by tropical trees, hiking trails wind by the Akaka Falls, which drop 420 spectacular feet into the Kolekole Stream below.

Left: Brilliant anthuriams thrive in the balmy climate of Hawaii's Puna District on the east coast. Anthuriam and orchid nurseries abound; the Big Island grows 93 percent of the state's anthuriams. These hardy flowers have longlasting blooms and grow wild as well.

Below: Almost hidden by a thick undergrowth of fern and bamboo, a stream winds its way over mossy rocks in Akaka Falls State Park. The morning air already hangs heavy with the rich smells of a tropical rain forest.

Sulphur steam rises above hardened lava in Kilauea's Halemaumau crater, creating an eerie effect that some attribute to the fire goddess, Pele.

Above: Liliuokalani Gardens Park on the shores of Hilo Bay was named after Hawaii's last monarch, Queen Liliuokalani, who ruled until 1893. This beautiful Japanese garden provides a five acre oasis in the busy city.
Below: The interior of St Benedict's Catholic Church at Honaunau on the Kona Coast presents an unusual blend of art styles. Called the Painted Church, its walls depict Biblical scenes while the ceiling portrays Hawaiian foliage and sky.
Opposite: The pristine appearance and lovely setting of St Peter's Catholic Church at Kahaluu Bay belie the fact that it was built on an ancient temple or *heiau* site.

Opposite: *Ki'i* figures stand guard in the City of Refuge at Honaunau, now a National Historic Park. Fugitives could find sanctuary and relief here.

Left: A cluster of papaya ripens in the sun.

Below: Hawaii provides rich grazing for its many cattle, first brought to the islands in 1793.

Right: Polynesian culture is evident during festivals, when flower *leis* and headdresses are donned.

Bottom: Ferns contrast with the bleak but awesome expanse of the Halemaumau Crater.

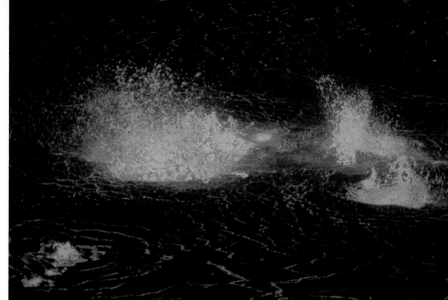

Left: The bleached remains of trees scorched by the eruption of Kilauea Iki in 1959 mark the landscape along Devastation Trail, an appropriately-named path half a mile long. The Kilauea Iki crater is east of the Kilauea Caldera.

Above and below: The dramatic eruptions of Kilauea in 1967, 1971 and 1984 filled the crater of Halemaumau with spewing, pressurized molten lava. The floor of the crater changes its depth with each eruption.

Right: A field of red and yellow poinsettias near the town of Captain Cook, where the explorer landed in 1779. These flowers are both brilliant and abundant on Hawaii, where most of them are of a rich-colored, double-headed variety.

Below: Rainbow Falls in Wailuku River State Park west of Hilo takes its name from the morning and afternoon rainbows that form in its mist. The refreshing air and exhilaration inspired by the falls are matched only by the striking beauty of the surrounding deep green foliage, punctuated with colorful flowers. In the foreground are torch ginger blooms and leaves. The torch ginger is commonly held to be the most magnificent of all the gingers.

Opposite: Canoeing is one of the most ancient Hawaiian sports. The sport is especially a part of Hawaii's roots, since the Polynesians who first settled the island arrived in 100-foot, double-hulled sailing canoes after an amazing journey of 2000 miles.

Left: Surfing is one of Hawaii's most popular sports today, as it was among the ancient Hawaiians, who loved to race and place bets on surfers. In the summer, surfing is best on Hawaii's south shores. The excitement and challenge of this incomparable sport is obviously addictive.

Above: Sailing is one of the best and most relaxing ways to appreciate Hawaii's beauty — tacking in an ocean breeze, skimming over sapphire-blue water, feeling the salty spray.
Below: Water skiing isn't the only type of skiing on Hawaii, as snow skiing reaches a new height on Mauna Kea's whitecapped peak.

Clouds linger in Haleakala Crater in Maui's Haleakala National Park,
blending with the muted colors of the cindercones.

Maui

Maui

Maui, the Valley Isle, is renowned for rolling foothills, grasslands, sugar cane and pineapple plantations and the beautiful Haleakala National Park. The second largest of the Hawaiian islands, Maui stretches 48 miles long and 26 miles wide for a total of 728 square miles. At an elevation above sea level of 10,000 feet, the highest on Maui, one can see both Molokai and Lanai. The historic city of Lahaina was once the capital of all Hawaii. In the nineteenth century Lahaina became the whaling capital of the Pacific – a favorite port of call for whaling ships. Many missionaries also made their homes in Lahaina, and clashes between whalers and missionaries have become legendary.

Herman Melville and Mark Twain both visited Maui and recorded their impressions for posterity. Today, the beautiful island offers ample opportunities for a leisurely life: camping, hiking, horseback riding, fishing, sailing, snorkeling, hunting, golfing, polo, tennis and winter whale-watching. The elegant Kaanapali Resort contains two famous golf courses. Scenic Hana Highway along the northern Hana Coast offers spectacular overlooks for picnics, extending almost to the lush Iao Valley Park, which separates East and West Maui.

Haleakala Crater, with unearthly cloud effects and breathtaking altitude, aptly translates as 'House of the Sun.' It is here that the silverswords grow – the only place in the world where their silvery spikes can be found. And it was here that Mark Twain camped, describing the view from the crater: 'The sea was spread abroad on every hand, its tumbled surface seeming only wrinkled and dimpled in the distance. A broad valley below appeared like an ample checker-board, its velvety green sugar plantations alternating with dun squares of barrenness and groves of trees diminished to mossy tufts.' Mark Twain was not the only one to be impressed with Haleakala; the National Park Service estimates that it is visited by more than 600,000 people a year.

The saying on Maui, *Ho'o kipa mai*, meaning 'come and be friendly,' sums up the island's philosophy very well. Maui's people are as hospitable as the mountains and valleys are enchanting. The casual *aloha*, uttered with warmth and sincerity, may do the soul more good than all the ocean views in the world.

Twisted branches frame a view of this beach on Maui, where one could be alone with only the sounds of surf and wind.

Left: Colorful windsurfers skim across the bay off Maui's coast. As in many other sea resorts, windsurfing has become one of most popular sports in Maui. Since temperatures rarely dip below the 65 degree mark, and usually hover in the eighties, windsurfing is enjoyed all year round.

Right: Swimmers splash about in the Ohe'O Stream in Heleakala National Park, in Maui's Kipahulu District. The shallow, protected waters offer a perfect bathing spot for families. Upstream of this spot, the sacred Ohe'O Gulch once provided bathing pools for Hawaiian royalty.

Below: A rainbow and palm tree enhance the idyllic setting for the golf course at Kaanapali. A major tourist attraction, the wealthy resort of Kaanapali was carved out of pineapple fields and a beautiful white sand coast. Elegant hotels and condominiums do not diminish the natural beauty of the area.

The luxurious Kaanapali Beach stretches for three miles along the famed resort area.

Below: Snorkling and skindiving are popular off the Maui coast where even beginners can see tropical fish and colorful coral gardens.
Bottom: The spirit of old Hawaii lives on in its outrigger canoes, gliding here amidst the lilypads.

Below: A Hawaiian fisherman checks his net in the glow of sunset. Although the native fisherman is a rarity now, many fish for sport.
Right: Yachts bob on the peaceful water in Lahaina Harbor in the afternoon sun. This harbor once serviced many whaling ship.

Twenty-one miles in circumference, the vast Haleakala Crater contains nine cinder cones. The sculptured terrain, painted in subtle hues, presents an unearthly picture.

Opposite: Surf crashes on the Ke'anae Peninsula on the east Maui coast. The rugged coast of black lava rocks has its own windswept beauty. Palm trees, described by Mark Twain as 'feather dusters hit by lightning,' act as a windbreak for the peninsula's native farmers.

Left: Silverswords grow on the rim of Haleakala, seen here at sunset with clouds grouping in the background. These rare plants are found only on Maui, where they grow for 20 years before sending up a stalk covered with purple and yellow flowers, and then die after a week or so. The ghostly spikes have a waxy coating to prevent water loss in this arid environment.

Below: According to island legend, it was from the heights of Haleakala that the Polynesian demigod Mauai captured the sun and made it promise to move more slowly across the sky. Here, sunrise glows in the crater, a sight described by Mark Twain as 'the sublimest spectacle I ever witnessed.'

Top: A pineapple field in West Maui. Molokai can be seen in the distance.
Above: Sugar cane thrives in Maui's temperate climate.

Opposite: Iao Stream cascades below Iao Needle, a volcanic monolith 2250 feet tall. Here Maui was defeated by Kamehameha I in a bloody battle.

Surf outlines Molokai's Kalaupapa Peninsula, where victims of leprosy were exiled in the mid-1880s. Fewer than 100 lepers remain at Kalaupapa, although they are legally free to leave.

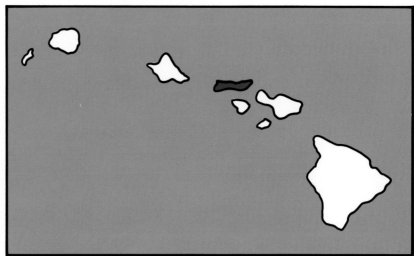

Molokai

Molokai, the Friendly Island, lies between Maui and Oahu in the island chain. Shaped like a slipper, the island is 37 miles long and ten miles wide, totalling 261 square miles. The island was created by the volcanic activities of Mauna Loa, Mauna Kamakou and Kauhako Volcano. The north of Molokai is mainly mountain range, while to the west lies the tableland of Mauna Loa. The eastern side of the island has few people and some early missionary churches in the New England style. Molokai's land varies from dry plains that barely support the lazily grazing cattle, to lush jungle areas cut through by foot and jeep paths, opening up now and then to a few cottages or a fishing shanty nestled under palm trees. A hike through one of Molokai's beautiful valleys can yield sights of ancient fish ponds built as early as the sixteenth century, a sacred *kukui* grove planted by a *kahuna* or priest, or vistas across the glittering sea to Maui, Oahu or Lanai. Fifth largest of the Hawaiian islands, Molokai is best known for its famed leper colony on Kalaupapa Peninsula. In the nineteenth century lepers were shipped here from the other islands and left to fend for themselves with little outside aid. In 1873, Father Damien de Veuster arrived at Kalaupapa, and he devoted his life to improving conditions of the colony, until he contracted the disease himself and died in 1889 at the age of 49. Molokai harbors a statue of the great man; the churches he built on the island remain as a testament to his dedication.

Molokai is gaining in popularity as more visitors to the islands discover its sleepy charm, slow-moving pace, gorgeous beaches, broad valleys and breathtaking waterfalls. Hunting and fishing on Molokai is unsurpassed, as is hiking in Halawa Valley. Some man-made fishing ponds, constructed by the ancient Hawaiians, still remain. Molokai's capital, Kaunakaki, once the shipping center for the island's pineapple industry, still has a busy wharf and a bustling market day every Saturday. The percentage of Molokai's population that is Hawaiian or part-Hawaiian is greater than that of any other island, which accounts for the nickname, 'the Friendly Isle.' From its lush tropical scenery to its sculptured coastline, Molokai is a place to be savored.

In an almost perfect Hawaiian landscape, sharply angled coconut palms are silhouetted against a colorful sky at twilight on the peaceful and deserted beach at Onealii, on the coast of Molokai.

Above: A ranch nestles in a fertile valley at the foot of furrowed mountain slopes in southeast Molokai. Many kinds of flowers and fruits grow wild in the valleys, including bananas, mountain apples, ginger, Java plum and guavas. Forests harbor eucalyptus and pine as well as *ohi'a* and ferns.

Below: The afterglow of sunset warms Molokai's north coast. Evenings on the island bring cool breezes and a respite from the day's activities with little nightlife.
Right: A gracefully-arching tree frames the mountains of Molokai, including Kamakou — at 4970 feet the highest point on the island.

Left: Surf hits the rugged coast at Moomomi Beach on Molokai's north shore. Located midway between Kalaupapa and Ilio Point, this beach is relatively isolated and untamed. True nature-lovers enjoy hiking around this unspoiled area where rippled sand dunes and fresh water pools are part of the attraction.

Right: A view of the spectacular Halawa Bay shows the mouth of Halawa Valley. Four miles long and half a mile wide, Halawa Valley features cascading waterfalls, fishponds, ancient *heiau* or temple sites and scenic backpacking trails.

Below: Our Lady of Sorrows Church at Kaluaaha was built by Father Damien in 1874. Situated in a palm grove with a mountain backdrop, the church has been recently restored and the well-kept grounds contribute to its peace and serenity. A statue of Father Damien stands in the pavilion nearby.

Surf and undertow create fleeting mosaics among the rocks at Lanai's Hulopoe Beach. The palm-fringed beach is an ideal spot for picnics.

Lanai

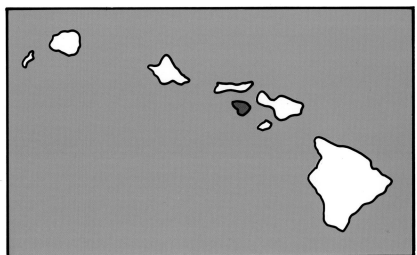

Lanai

Located south of Molokai and west of Maui, the small and unassuming island of Lanai lies — all 141 square miles of it — in the blue Pacific. Seventeen miles long and 13 miles wide, Lanai is shaped like a pear. With only a small population, Lanai is sixth in size of the Hawaiian islands. Reaching a height of 3370 feet in one continuous swell of land, Lanai translates, appropriately, as 'the hump.' Pineapple fields account for 15,000 of Lanai's acres, most of which are owned by Dole Company. Upwards of a million pineapples a day are yielded during the harvest season. Lanai City, with its quaint evergreens and cultivated flowers, is an idyllic company town. Lanai's east coast is scored by deep gulches, while the west coast is bordered by cliffs. North to south, the island slopes in a relatively smooth ridge.

Legend has it that Maui's King Kaalaneo's son, Laululaao, was exiled to Lanai after one of his many pranks. Ghosts and evil spirits made the island unfit for humans, and Laululaao was expected to die. But with courage and cunning, he defeated the evil spirits one by one, making the island livable and becoming a hero in the process. It is true that Lanai was the last of the Hawaiian islands to be settled. The fishermen and farmers who made the island their home first arrived in the early fifteenth century. The wild beauty of Lanai attracted Kamehameha, who had a resort here. In 1835 missionaries arrived in Lanai, and were followed years later by Mormons.

Lanai is off the beaten tourist path. Its rugged and rocky features, dusty red earth and few roads encourage the visitor who likes to rough it. But the island has much to offer, including a lovely swimming beach, sailing, camping, hiking and golfing. The naturalist or historian will enjoy searching for the marine fossils at Hulopoe Bay or for the odd petroglyphs found all over the island. Remains of ships, fallen victim to the treacherous reef, give a ghostly air to Shipwreck Beach. Garden of the Gods, a geological oddity, is strewn with lava boulders and multi-colored sands. With its vegetation ranging from dainty to scruffy, its busy harbor and its colorful landscape, Lanai remains unspoiled — a relic of the Hawaii of yesteryear.

Lava rocks on Molokai form the foreground of this view of Lanai across the Kaholi Channel.

Left: Beached timbers washed up on the shore lend a plaintive air to Shipwreck Beach, where many unfortunate vessels were washed onto the reef by fierce tradewinds. Most of the wrecks are from the days of sailing ships. The island of Molokai lies across the Kaholi Channel.

Above: This deep valley carved in the mountains on the eastern side of Lanai shows the red soil so characteristic of the island. The gulches and ravines make rough but rewarding hiking.

Below: Lava boulders, seemingly deposited from the sky, lie strewn about in Garden of the Gods. Located seven miles from Lanai City in northwest Lanai, the unusual landscape is one of distorted lava formations wrought by the forces of erosion. The island of Molokai can be seen in the distance, its hazy blueness contrasting the weathered earthtones on Lanai.

Oahu

Waikiki highrises brighten up the night in Honolulu. The glamorous, boisterous night life of the city is one of Oahu's main attractions.

Oahu

Oahu, the main island, is the hub of Hawaii. Forty miles long and 26 miles wide, the island encompasses 607 square miles and the vast majority of Hawaii's population, numbering 886,000. Hawaii's most wellknown and frequently-visited places – Honolulu, Waikiki, Diamond Head, Pearl Harbor – are all found on Oahu, which entertains about four million tourists each year. Besides these popular sights, Oahu harbors a wealth of historic and natural landmarks. Located between Kauai and Molokai, the island was formed by two volcanic domes, the Koolau Range, stretching southeast to northwest, and the western Waianae Mountains. Conquered by Kamehameha in 1795, Oahu honors the great king with a regal statue of bronze. Oahu's seaside summer palace and fine harbors made it a favorite among the islands even in the 1800s, when the crater of Diamond Head was used a a virtually inpenetrable defense fort. Furrowed mountains and valleys contain lush rain forests. The Waianae Mountains and coastline offer superb camping, swimming and surfing. Oahu reaches its highest elevation – 4020 feet – at Mount Kaala's summit. Waimea Falls Park in the Koolau foothills contains a wide range of plant life, from mango trees to guava. In the quiet northern region of Oahu, small farms take advantage of the fertile valley soil. One can never travel too far on this island without encountering one of its many parks and gardens, with tree-shaded arbors, ponds and pleasant picnic spots. Koko Head and Koko Crater, east of Diamond Head, form one of these parks. Japanese shrines and Buddhist temples coexist with churches, testifying to the island's interethnic quality. But Honolulu is the greatest unifier to east and west, old and new. The Honolulu Harbor, once filled with whaling and merchant ships, now shelters gleaming yachts. Honolulu's elegant Iolani Palace, once the residence of Hawaiian royalty, is a contrast to the modern State Capitol building, famous for its volcano-shaped crown of glass and concrete. Chinatown, twice burnt to the ground and twice rebuilt, offers open-air markets and a festive atmosphere. The University of Hawaii and Aloha Stadium nestle inland of Waikiki, and it is not far from there to Pearl Harbor, where the battleships *Arizona* and *Utah* still lie underwater. Oahu contains all the elements of Hawaii on its well-travelled shores. Even at raucous Waikiki, the breezes at sunrise seem to bring the faint stirring of drumbeats heard long ago.

The familiar sight of Diamond Head, with Waikiki Beach curving out to meet it. In the foreground is the Sheraton Royal Hawaiian Hotel, otherwise known as the Pink Palace. Highrise hotels crowd Waikiki, where 25,000 hotel rooms await the weary traveler. The beach here is a favorite spot for meeting people or catching a quick tan.

Below: Clouds drift lazily over the crater of Diamond Head and Waikiki, as a boat heads back to harbor after a morning cruise.

Bottom: Built in 1927, the Sheraton Royal Hawaiian Hotel quickly became one of the most popular resorts in the islands. The Pink Palace, with its exquisite setting and period decor, still woos many an island guest.

Right: Both the Waikiki and Hawaii Yacht Clubs are located in the picturesque Ala Wai Yacht Basin.

Top: Makapuu Beach at Honolulu's eastern end is a favorite spot for body-surfing and escaping from the crowds at Waikiki. The flat island offshore is called Kaohikaipu Island; the larger one is Manana, also known as Rabbit Island.

Above: The traditional *luau* is an integral part of Hawaiian social life. The pig, filled with heated rocks and wrapped in leaves, is buried with fish and yams in a hole lined with wood and steaming lava rock. Hours later the food, distinctly flavored, is unearthed and served.

Above: Dressed in bright *mu'umu'us* and garlanded with *leis*, women perform at a concert at the Waikiki Shell.

Left: Children ride a float in the Aloha Week Parade, which takes place in Hololulu in October. Colorful and festive, the parade is flavored with elements of Polynesian culture.

Below: A colorful pageant with the famed Hawaiian feather headdresses takes place in the Polynesian Cultural Center.

Right: Tourists watch a procession of the Polynesian-style double-hulled canoes.

Left: The cultural diversity of Hawaii is evident in its variety of religious structures. The stately Mormon Temple, built in 1919 in the Mormon settlement at Laie, is situated close to the Polynesian Cultural Center.

Above: Hawaii's first church — Kawaiahao Church — was built of coral blocks in 1841 in Honolulu on the site of Hawaii's first mission. The church's Sunday services are conducted in English and Hawaiian.

Below: The serene Byodo-In Temple, situated at Kaneohe in Valley of the Temples Memorial Park, is a replica of the temple in Kyoto. The 2000-foot-high Koolau cliffs serve as a dramatic backdrop.

A quiet sunset at Kaena Point, with the Waianae Mountains receding into dusk.

Above: Honolulu's $30 million Aloha Stadium was completed in 1975, Located near Pearl Harbor, the stadium hosts the annual Hula Bowl. *Below*: The only royal palace in the United States, Iolani Palace was completed in 1882 and briefly housed Hawaiian royalty.

Right: This gilded bronze statue of King Kamehameha, unifier of the Hawaiian islands, stands before the Judiciary Building in Honolulu. The statue depicts the conqueror wearing a feather cloak and helmet, a spear in his left hand and his right arm extended in a gesture of peace.

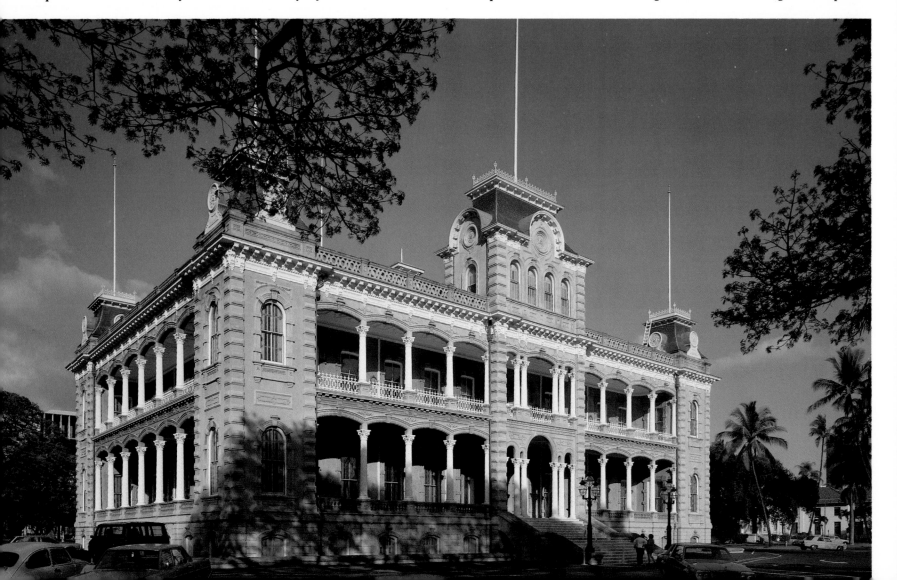

Left: Built in Scotland in 1878, the restored *Falls of Clyde* survives today as the world's only full-rigged, four-masted sailing ship. Located at Pier 5 in Honolulu Harbor, the ship is a maritime museum.

Above: Hawaiian women dance the ancient *hula* in front of a thatch hut during the Kodak Hula Show in Kapiolani Park. The colorful show has been a regular attraction since it was first staged in 1937.

Below: A flame dancer performs on the sand stage at the Polynesian Cultural Center. Since 1964 the center has hosted shows of ancient sports and arts.

Right: Blowing a conch shell signifies the start of festivities.

IN THESE GARDENS ARE RECORDED
THE NAMES OF AMERICANS
WHO GAVE THEIR LIVES
IN THE SERVICE OF THEIR COUNTRY
AND WHOSE EARTHLY RESTING PLACE
IS KNOWN ONLY TO GOD
★ Indicates MEDAL OF HONOR Award

Left: Diamond Head is actually an extinct volcano from which a superb view of Honolulu and Waikiki can be seen.
Top: Hanauma Bay, 'the curved bay,' is an extinct crater eroded by the sea.
Above: The Punchbowl Crater was designated the National Memorial Cemetery of the Pacific in 1949. More than 22,000 servicemen killed in World Wars I and II, and the Korean and Vietnam Wars, are buried here.
Right: The State Capitol Building's columns suggest palm trees.

Honolulu's highrises reflect the glow of sunset, with Diamond Head in the background.

Opposite top: Plumeria blossoms grow on the tree's forked branches, which bloom continually from spring until winter. The fragrant, long-lasting flowers are favorites for making leis.

Opposite middle: The beautiful and dainty Vanda Orchid hybrid is also used for making leis. Many are grown for shipment to the mainland.

Opposite bottom: The brilliant Bird of Paradise enlivens many Hawaiian parks.

Left: Dramatic lighting characterizes this spectacular view of the southern end of the Koolau Range, seen from Nu'uanu Pali State Park. The mountains' imposing green and brown walls loom over the fertile coastal plains and small villages nestled at their feet.

Top: Diamond Head serves as a somber backdrop for the brilliance of Waikiki at night. Flood-lit palm trees sway in the cool ocean breeze as the calm water reflects Waikiki's many lights, adding excitement to the night time festivities.

Above: A surfer rests on his board at Sunset Beach on Oahu's north shore. Located between Waialee and Waimea, this is one of Hawaii's most dangerous beaches because of its enormous waves, but it also has the state's finest surfing.

At 7:55 am on 7 December 1941 Pearl Harbor was devastated by the Japanese attack which initiated World War II in the Pacific Theater, causing 3435 casualties and crippling the US Navy. Designated a national historic site, the memorials at Pearl Harbor are visited by more than a million people a year.

Top left: The *Arizona* Memorial, a white concrete bridge designed by Alfred Preis, spans the hulk of the sunken USS *Arizona*, in which 1102 sailers are entombed.

Above left: The anchor raised from the hulk of the USS *Arizona*, on exhibit at the memorial.

Left: The superstructure of the USS *Arizona* still rises above the waves.

Above: A side view of the *Arizona* Memorial, to which the Navy operates a shuttle boat for visitors. The memorial was funded in part by Elvis Presley, whose benefit concert in 1961 raised over $62,000.

Right: On a marble wall inside the *Arizona* Memorial, the names of the dead below are permanently inscribed.

Far right: A painting on the wall inside the *Arizona* Memorial depicts the battleship as she appeared before her sinking.

Kauai

Kauai, the Garden Island, lies 72 miles northwest of Oahu. The oldest of the Hawaiian islands, Kauai's 548 square miles support a population of about 40,000. The first of the islands to be settled by the Polynesians, Kauai also has the distinction of being the only island never conquered by Kamehameha. Captain Cook anchored at this island first, and legend has it that other visitors, the Menehune, also enjoyed the islands's hospitality. Various dams, ditches and trails, many of unique construction, are attributed to this legendary race of little people, two feet tall, who worked at night to create these vast projects.

Mount Waialeale rises to 5170 feet in the center of Kauai. Receiving 451 inches of rainfall annually, it is the wettest spot in the world. The spectacular mountains, canyons cut with rivers and sparkling waterfalls, lush jungles and extraordinary parks and gardens earn Kauai its epithet, the Garden Island. In addition to harboring practically every form of plant life found on the Hawaiian islands, Kauai also has a vast collection of rare plants and animals which are found nowhere else on earth. The fourth largest Hawaiian island, Kauai offers unspoiled hiking and camping grounds and beautiful vistas. The northwest Na Pali Coast is reknowned for its steep cliffs and ravines. Kokee State Park lies inland of here at the northern end of Waimea Canyon, which cuts up the island from Waimea on the island's southwest shore. The canyon's verdant greenery is contrasted by deep red soil bared by landslides, and the crisp air makes the vistas all the more exhilarating. East of Waimea, the Old West-style town of Hanapepe charms visitors with its false-front buildings. Further to the east, the old plantation town of Lihue, with a population of 4000, contains German and New England style architecture, Japanese gardens and the delightful Kauai Museum. East and north of Lihue, Kauai reveals its various industries in its sugar cane fields, poi factories, macademia nut farms, taro patches and resorts. Lumahai Beach, well-known for its distinctive beauty, is found on the north shore. With its generous life-giving rainfall and the rich diversity of its landscapes and wildlife, Kauai is Hawaii's greenest and most refreshing island.

This page: The Spouting Horn sends a spray of salt water into the sunsetlit sky. The geyser is caused by the sea being forced through a lava tube.

Pages 82 and 83: The beautiful Fern Grotto filled with many exotic and specimen plants, typifies Kauai's beauty.

Opposite: Kilauea Lighthouse is located on the northernmost point of Kauai in the Kilauea Point National Wildlife Refuge in the Hanalei District. Now automated, the lighthouse is a beacon for ships coming from the Orient; it contains the world's largest clamshell lens. The bluff which it occupies offers superb views.

Left: Taro thrives in the rich soil of the Hanalei Valley in Kauai's northern region. Taro is used for making poi, a sticky, purple, Hawaiian food that is eaten, preferably, with the fingers. A staple in the Hawaiian diet, poi is made from the plant's roots, pounded into a paste and mixed with water.

Below: The silvery ribbon of the Hanelei River cuts through the Hanelei Valley, the wettest and greenest part of Kauai. Taro patches and small farms form a quilted pattern, stretching to the foot of the mountains' green foothills.

The beach at Haena Bay on Kauai's north shore separates jagged mountains from crystal-clear water.

Left: An *ohia lehua* tree frames this impressive view of the Kalalau Valley in the northwest.
Above: The popular Lumaha'i Beach on the island's north coast is framed by *hala* trees.
Right: The Menehune Ditch in Waimea Valley is attributed by local legend to the Menehune dwarfs.
Below: Sugar cane grows in the morning sun in the Koloa District.

Below: The spectacular folds and ridges of Waimea Canyon seen from the lookout in this state park are breathtaking to behold. The canyon stretches from the southwest coast north to the Kokee Plateau. The 2857-foot-deep gorge is reminiscent of the Grand Canyon.

Right: Wailua River State Park is as rich in history as it is in beauty. Located on the east coast, the park contains the ruins of a temple of refuge, boulders with petroglyphs, royal burial grounds and ancient *heiaus*. The Wailua Falls drop 50 feet to a natural swimming pool.

This coconut grove on the east coast was once a royal enclave. The first settlers landed near here.

Coastline palms at sunset at Kukui'ula Bay